>>> **e-guidelines** 9

Supporting adult learners with dyslexia: harnessing the power of technology

Sally McKeown

promoting adult learning

ⓝiace
promoting adult learning

©2006 National Institute of Adult Continuing Education
(England and Wales)
21 De Montfort Street
Leicester
LE1 7GE
Company registration no. 2603322
Charity registration no. 1002775

NIACE has a broad remit to promote lifelong learning
opportunities for adults. NIACE works to develop increased
participation in education and training, particularly for those who
do not have easy access because of class, gender, age, race,
language and culture, learning difficulties or disabilities, or
insufficient financial resources.

You can find NIACE online at **www.niace.org.uk**

Cataloguing in Publication Data

A CIP record of this title is available from the British Library

Designed and typeset by Book Production Services, London
Printed and bound in the UK by Latimer Trend

ISBN: 1 86201 293 8
       978 1 86201 293 6

Contents

1   Introduction   1

2   What is dyslexia?   3

    Behaviour   7

3   How do people learn?   9

4   Be prepared   15

    First impressions matter!   15

    Planning ahead   17

    Assessment   20

      Access arrangements   20

5   Making reading easier   23

    Keep all your handouts on electronic files   24

    Do not use justified text   24

    Give a choice of colours where possible   25

    Make web pages easier to read   26

    Use sans serif fonts   28

    Don't print text over images   28

    Use styles and headings as signposts   29

    Do not pack in too much information   30

    Use screen tips   31

    Provide a text-to-speech facility   32

    Useful sources of support   33

6   Does it have to be reading and writing?   33

    Working with the text   33

    Diagrams *v.* text   35

    Keep instructions simple   36

    Combine different media   36

    Sorting activities   38

    Using PowerPoint as a visual prompt   38

    Labelling diagrams   39

    Cloze   39

    Drag and drop   40

    Webquest   41

    Further information   43

7	Supporting writing	44
	Planning	44
	Writing	44
	Points to consider	49
8	Good skills for learners	51
	How to change colours and fonts	52
	Paste special	52
	AutoSummarise	52
	Highlighter	53
	Spike	53
	Using bullet points or numbering	54
	Spell checker	54
	Thesaurus	55
	AutoCorrect	56
	Google toolbar	56
9	Conclusion	58
10	References	59
	Organisations	59
	Sites	60
	Books and articles	61
	Contacts for software mentioned in the text	62

This book has a different design than other e-guidelines. It incorporates features intended to increase readability for readers with dyslexia. As well as using a sans serif typeface and a modified colour scheme, we have cropped and re-shaped details from screen grabs, rather than using untouched pictures.

1

Introduction

Computers are a vital part of our lives today, with increasing numbers of people having access to them through community centres, libraries and the workplace, as well as at home.

Technology offers a host of services unimaginable a few years ago. People routinely send e-mails, look up local history information on the web, download music, book holidays and even do the shopping from the comfort of their nearest computer.

As a result of wider computer access, learners now expect to have access to a range of electronic and multimedia resources, as well as the tutors' expertise. E-learning brings together ICT (information and communication technology) skills and learning content. It can be used for distance learning or in face-to-face classes where the tutor incorporates digitally produced resources into the learning process.

This booklet provides information and guidance for tutors in any subject area who want to offer good-quality support for dyslexic learners. Although you might think it unlikely that someone with reading and writing problems would want to sign up for a course where they would need to be reading text on screen or using a keyboard to enter information, many people with dyslexia have found that the computer actually open doors to learning and can help them minimise, if not overcome, their issues with text.

With the right support and training, they can learn to take control of their own computer interface, setting colours and fonts to make text clearer or use a speech engine to read text back to them so they can concentrate on the meaning instead of individual words.

Learning should be an active process and should *engage* people. E-learning is particularly good for this, because learners have to make and register choices; they get a response that may lead them to take a different route, which may turn out to be better for them.

e-learning can:

> attract learners
> create a positive learning environment
> enhance teaching methods
> empower learners
> improve literacy skills and communication skills
> widen the range of learners engaging in adult and continuing education
> extend the range of teaching and learning methods
> motivate learners
> give learners transferable skills
> offer extra skills for employment

2

What is dyslexia?

Many people used to think that there was no such thing as dyslexia. It was dismissed as a 'literacy difficulty for the middle classes'. While there are still a few who claim that dyslexia is a myth, the last 10–15 years have seen a considerable amount of research on the subject.

You might therefore think that by now there is an accepted definition of exactly what dyslexia is, but as the following headlines, collected on the Literacy Trust website (**www.literacytrust.org.uk**) show, the debate continues:

'Faulty gene gives clue to tackling dyslexia' (2003)

'Balance treatment hailed as a success by researchers' (2002)

'Study suggests eye patch could help dyslexics to read' (2000)

'Eating fish could help dyslexia' (2004)

'Breath test can identify dyslexia' (2002)

'Intensive training can 'jump-start' dyslexics' brains' (2004)

Dyslexia is often characterised as difficulty in reading, writing, spelling and/or expressing thoughts on paper. There are many distinctions and definitions; for example:

Language processing difficulty

Poor phonological awareness; difficulty in repeating polysyllabic words; poor short-term memory

Magnocellular deficit

Difficulty in integrating information from different sensory pathways, causing problems in distinguishing similar sounds and quickly changing patterns of letters as the eye scans words – in research this is referred to as the 'transient hypothesis'

Visual dyslexia Difficulty in forming a stable image of the word, or in processing the shape and orientation of letters and words

Memory and memory allocation problems

Too much emphasis on decoding letters and words and too little on understanding the text

Poor automaticity

Difficulty in developing skills for reading such as eye movements, auditory skills and articulation skills

Inability to learn and implement new strategies

Difficulty in adapting to phonologically irregular words, leading to an over-reliance on phonics

A non-specialist overview of the different theories of and approaches to dyslexia is given in *A Framework for Understanding Dyslexia*, a research project jointly led by the Learning and Skills Development Agency and NIACE (DfES 2004): available at **http://www.dfes.gov.uk/readwriteplus/understandingdyslexia/**

One thing that all definitions agree upon is that dyslexia is a persistent condition that cannot be accounted for by explanations such as hearing or sight loss.

Dyslexia does not just affect literacy however. Each individual will have a unique pattern of difficulties which may include motor skills or auditory or visual processing. In addition to the mechanics of reading, writing and spelling, learners may also experience issues with:

> visual discrimination and perception
> pronunciation, particularly words of three or more syllables
> auditory discrimination:

Sue, a tutor in Bedfordshire, said her student Bernard has really poor word recognition skills. 'After months of trying, he confuses *what* and *want*, *with* and *which*. It's as if he doesn't see the middle of words. We have started using a talking word processor so he can hear what the words say and read along with the text.'

> sequencing
> left and right:

Lesley goes to line dancing. She loves the music and has a great sense of rhythm, but is often going the wrong way as she is slow to respond to shouts of 'Left!' and 'Right!'. 'It was more of a difficulty when I was younger. In secondary school I never mastered *droit* and *gauche* in French even though I could translate them OK. I know the difference between left and right but it's not automatic, so I end up being one beat behind everyone else. It's really irritating.'

> long-term and short-term memory
> time management
> organisational skills:

Jayne is now a play leader in Hertfordshire. She did a degree in art but always found writing problematic. She could not maintain her portfolio of work for her play leader qualification, so decided to tackle her writing difficulties head on. Diagnosed at the age of 40 as having dyslexia, she has begun to take an interest in different software packages for learners with dyslexia and loves the mind mapping software. 'I used to try to write a plan and then flesh it out bit by bit, and it would be such a muddle. Now I put everything into a mind map, move the pieces around and decide what I am going to throw away. Then I have a proper structure and can do that planning bit they used to nag me about when I was at college. It all seems quite straightforward now.'

While there is much that you as a tutor can do to help your learners develop skills that will be beneficial in their day-to-day life, do remember that your role is to use technology and e-learning to maximise their abilities in your own field of study. Learners have come to learn your subject, not to be given lots of drill and practice literacy activities. Over the years they will have developed skills and strengths that can be put to good use in your classroom. Some also come with preferences about how they like materials presented and a range of different learning strategies:

Kathy likes to have written directions to get from one part of town to another. If faced with a map, she translates it into sentences, 'Turn right into Bedford Street, left at the end of the road, turn right and first right.' Jack is a visual learner and prefers maps. Faced with a string of directions, he loses the thread and gets very frustrated, but he has an almost photographic memory for maps and a fair sense of direction.

Jack and Kathy want to go to an antique fair at Olympia, London W14, and needs to find a hotel. Kathy types 'Hotel Olympia UK' into a search engine. Jack opens Google Map, types in 'Hotel W!4' and gets a map showing the location of the hotels. There are hot links enabling him to get further information.

Jack and Kathy reached the same (or similar!) destinations but went by different routes which worked best for them.

Behaviour

While many learners with dyslexia have above-average ability, they often lack self-esteem. Sometimes early schooling experiences had such a negative effect that they have lost confidence in their ability to undertake new learning. In some cases young people with dyslexia have become de-motivated as this extract from *The Guardian* shows:

A study carried out by the British Dyslexia Association [BDA] with the Youth Offending Team (YOT) in Bradford suggests that over half of young offenders are dyslexic (as opposed to 10% of the general population). And the more serious the offence, or the greater the number of offences, the higher the likelihood that the offender is dyslexic.

It has long been known that most young offenders have difficulties with literacy. 'Among our 15 and 16-year-olds,' says Paul O'Hara, Bradford YOT manager, 'a reading age of eight or nine is normal; seven is not uncommon. Many are not in school because they have been excluded or have dropped out. They are not part of mainstream society. They see themselves as outsiders and one thing leads to another.

(Guardian, 16 June 2004)

However, it would be wrong to suggest that people with dyslexia are more likely to drop out of education and turn to a life of crime. While the above figures from the BDA are alarming, it must be noted that there is also an increase in the numbers of students in universities who have dyslexia. People with dyslexia are very difficult to categorise.

Key points

> Dyslexia is more than a reading and writing difficulty.
> Dyslexia is a persistent condition.
> Dyslexic learners may have experienced frustrations in education if they did not receive the right support.
> Learners are individuals, not an example of a theory.
> e-learning and technology can offer access to subjects in new and interesting ways that are not necessarily text-dependent.
> If you suspect that a learner may have dyslexia, you should refer them to a specialist who can screen and assess them.

3

How do people learn?

When learners come to enrol and start a new course, they bring with them a lot of strengths and weaknesses. They may be nervous and worried about whether they will be able to keep up with the course; they may also be inspired by their passions and enthusiasm. Practitioners and organisers need to look at the whole person.

As well as getting information from reading and writing, people learn by:

> looking
> listening
> trying things out
> fitting new information into background knowledge
> anecdotal information
> discussion
> analysis
> reflection
> working with others
> making decisions

Most tutors are aware of the Visual Auditory and Kinaesthetic (VAK) styles of learning and try to involve a range of activities in their classes that will meet different learners' needs. However, VAK is only part of the story.

If you talk to people who do Sudoku, you will find that some work it out by listing the missing numbers and seeing where they might fit, while others can 'see' patterns and tell at a glance which line is lacking a particular number. Similarly, when

9

doing jigsaw puzzles, some start by finding all the straight edges, building a frame and then filling it in, while others look for a part of the picture that is easy to distinguish, perhaps because of colour or pattern, and find the pieces to create it. **There is no one right way of doing things.**

	9		4		5	3		
	4			6	3			
		8				5		
		7		8			1	
3							9	
1			6		5			
	2				7			
		9	1			6		
		3	7		6	9		

In 1981 Roger Sperry won the Nobel Peace Prize for his experiments on left-brain and right-brain hemisphere brain functions. He discovered that most of us use both sides of our brain but have a bias to one side or the other.

Try this quiz:

Left brain	Yes/No	Right brain	Yes/No
Are you organised?	☐ ☐	Do you do things on the spur of the moment?	☐ ☐
Are you a worrier?	☐ ☐		
Are you a planner?	☐ ☐	Are you often late?	☐ ☐
Do you like written directions?	☐ ☐	Do you do things when they occur to you rather than in a fixed order?	☐ ☐
Do you work through things methodically?	☐ ☐	Are you very easy going?	☐ ☐
		Are you a daydreamer?	☐ ☐
		Do you prefer a map?	☐ ☐
		Do you rely on bright ideas?	☐ ☐

If you answered yes to most of the questions in the left-hand column, you are a predominantly left-brained person. The left brain hemisphere specialises in logical, analytical and linear thinking and is a word- and language-based approach to information. If the right-hand column describes you more accurately, then the right-brain hemisphere is probably dominant: this specialises in intuitive, perceptual thinking. You will see patterns but might be hard put to explain them to others. Musical ability and abstract thinking are also features of right-brained people.

Being left- or right-brained is neither an advantage nor a drawback, but it has implications for the way people learn, the strategies they need to develop and the way we use computers and software to support them.

Left brain emphasises:	Right brain emphasises:
Language	Images
Rules and grammar	Awareness of shape
Mathematical formulae	Appreciation of patterns
Numbers	Able to work in three dimensions
Sequences	Rhythm and musical appreciation
Linearity	Seeing the whole picture
Analysis	

While there is no direct correlation between right-hemisphere dominance and dyslexia, we find that many learners with dyslexia tend to be right-brained individuals. At the same time, we are beginning to find that the best multimedia programmers are right-brained: they are able to operate in nonlinear ways and see patterns and links that are not apparent to left-brained individuals. That is perhaps why concept mapping works so well for them.

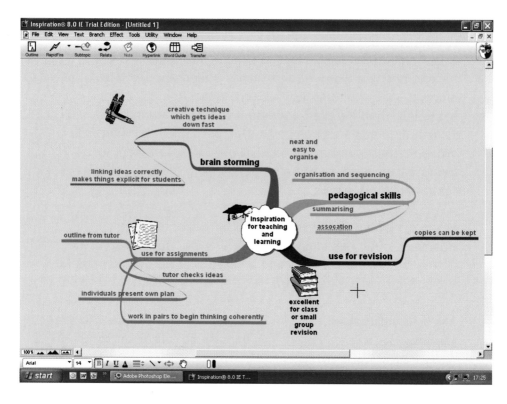

Ellen Lessner from Abingdon and Witney College is certain that mind mapping software promotes independence and encourages responsibility:

'I teach study skills to Access students, and one of first sessions (after assessing and discussion learning styles) is about using assistive software. I use the session as an informal diagnostic tool. You can easily see who can summarise, link sequentially, etc., by watching how learners use mapping software. For adult returners, many of whom are undiagnosed dyslexics, using visual skills in an academic setting is an eye opener and very liberating. They see the sense of it and have fun with it.'

Some argue that people have different approaches to the technology itself: that left-brained individuals prefer the structure of PCs, while right-brained people have a great affection for the Apple Mac.

Daphne, an E-Guide from Essex, has first-hand experience of dyslexia. Sometimes when she is tired she finds that her brain makes anagrams of words and she finds it hard to make sense of what she is reading. She has found that the interface and operating system of an Apple Mac is much easier for her to use. 'You just look at it and you can *see* how it works. Microsoft Office for Mac has far fewer distractions, and you don't have to drill down so many levels to get to the bit you want. Drag and drop is simpler, and when you plug in a camera it just opens up and doesn't ask you lots of questions. When I get stuck I have to remember to sit back and relax and look at it and wait to see how to do it, and Mac help is brilliant and uses very few words – only the right ones.'

Daphne has been impressed with the Minimac at £350. It looks like a small biscuit tin, is A5 size, made of brushed aluminium and has the basic Mac operating system. It is designed to appeal to the ipod market and comes with a modem, iphoto and itunes.
(see **http://store.apple.com/Apple/WebObjects/ukstore/**).

Ron Davis (1997), author of *The Gift of Dyslexia*, believes that dyslexia 'is something special that enhances the individual', and that such individuals have a number of talents:

> They can utilize the brain's abilities to alter and create perceptions (the primary ability).
> They are highly aware of the environment.
> They are more curious than average.
> They think mainly in pictures instead of words.
> They are highly intuitive and insightful.
> They think and perceive multi-dimensionally (using all the senses).
> They can experience thought as reality.
> They have vivid imaginations (see **http://www.dyslexia.com/bookstore/firstchapter.htm**).

Key points

> Learners with dyslexia have different approaches to learning.
> People with dyslexia may choose different paths to reach a goal.
> Dyslexia is not a handicap: inappropriate teaching can make it so.
> There are advantages to having dyslexia.

4

Be prepared

Under Part 4 of the Disability Discrimination Act (DDA) (2002), practitioners and managers have a responsibility to all disabled people – not just those who are already coming to classes, but all those who might choose to come in the future. A 'disability', as defined under the DDA, is a physical or mental impairment that has a substantial and long-term adverse effect on a person's ability to carry out formal day-to-day activities. Under the Act, dyslexia usually counts as a disability if it affects an individual's ability to concentrate or learn.

What this means is that teachers need to make good provision for those who have dyslexia: getting in a supply of 'Post-its' for mind mapping and different coloured paper for printing out; and thinking about how materials are prepared and stored – are they in a filing cabinet with an A–Z index, or on a Virtual Learning Environment (VLE) with a search facility? (See *A Framework for Understanding Dyslexia*, DfES 2004.)

First impressions matter!

Make dyslexic class members feel welcome. See them not as a problem, but as a resource that will bring different skills and strengths to the group.

At the initial meeting with a dyslexic or at the first class:
> Look.
> Listen.
> Learn.
> Don't make assumptions about where difficulties will lie.

> Remember, you may know a lot about dyslexia in general, but you are not an expert on how it affects an individual.
> Ask questions: what have they learnt successfully and how did they do it?
> Listen to answers: if they found it easy to learn to drive, perhaps they learn best by doing.
> Find out whether they have already used a computer.
> Don't rush to a suggest a solution.
> Find a way to alter your teaching style or materials in a way that will help them.
> Remember that it is not the job of practitioners or managers to diagnose dyslexia: know when to refer for extra help.

At the 'Print Out Your Future' (POYF) project in Leeds, tutors set out to build confidence.

'It was important to keep in touch. We started with mobile phones and visits from the outreach worker, but as the project went on e-mail became more important.

Valerie had suffered bullying and verbal abuse at work for years. People picked on her and told her she was 'thick', and she came to believe them. She was screened for dyslexia and came to see that she was not a failure, but just needed different forms of teaching and support. Val became much more confident and assertive and, with union backing, brought a case against the bullies.

Brenda Barnett, project manager

Sometimes you may see dyslexia occurring in families. Brothers and sisters may have shared similar issues or particular ways of learning. Family learning centres may liaise between schools and ACL as this example shows:

'In my experience, there is often a correlation between children's difficulties and those of their parents: this is seen most clearly in spelling problems, although the adult checklist we use highlights other areas probably not considered before.

'Many parents who are not too worried about their own difficulties will be far more focused on their child's needs, perhaps remembering their own feelings of failure at school. They may not wish at this time to pursue a diagnosis for themselves. The fact that they themselves have coped with life, despite having dyslexic difficulties, should be an encouragement that their children will get through their difficulties, too.

'We at City College tend to use particular sessions to draw out strategies for dyslexic difficulties, e.g. spelling, learning to read, listening skills, more advanced reading skills. These highlight issues for both children and adults.'

Anne Hughes, family learning tutor/dyslexia support at Southampton City College

Planning ahead

Practitioners and managers will need to plan ahead to provide appropriate support. You will need to be familiar with a wide span of resources relating to your topic – paper-based, electronic and activity-based. Remember that not everyone will get ideas and inspiration from the same materials.

Teaching will need to be differentiated by resource, support and response:

Resources Does everyone need to start form the same place? Might there be a more motivating set of resources for some learners such as pictures, videos or sound files? Can the core content be reduced? Can it be presented differently – as a slide show, or on a CD-ROM to take away? Can technology provide a better way of accessing resources?

Support e-learning lends itself to individual and small-group work. Often the tutor will be wandering around the room offering assistance to individuals; so it will be relatively easy to see who can't remember/understand/concentrate when everyone else is getting on. Might support be best coming in the form of pair-work?

Response In the old days staff kept records of marks. These days they are more likely to be ticking competencies. Do learners need a lot of short tasks or a longer piece they can get their teeth into? What are the alternatives in your subject to a printout that can go in a portfolio? Will the awarding body accept alternatives?

Think about these different tasks and decide whether a manager should do them, or a teacher, or both:

	Practitioner	Manager
Look up websites about dyslexia.		
Obtain and read the TechDis Staff Pack *Dyslexia and the use of assistive technology.* **http://www.techdis.ac.uk/resources/sites/ staffpacks/index.xml**		
Find out about exam arrangements.		
Ensure that teaching staff know how to change font sizes, typefaces and colours.		
Ensure that tutors can change background colours in Word and PowerPoint.		
Plan for ways of assessment that are not text-based.		

	Practitioner	Manager
Obtain and read the TechDis Staff Pack *e-Assessment.* **http://www.techdis.ac.uk/resources/sites/ staffpacks/index.xml**		
Audit software to see how useful it will be for devising activities and resources for learners with dyslexia.		
Ensure access to digital cameras.		
Ensure access to voice recorders/ microphones/MP3 players.		
Encourage staff to keep all handouts and materials electronically		
Establish what interactive software is available – Hot Potatoes? PowerPoint? SmartBoard? Word and Excel?		
Provide headphones so that learners can listen to text being read aloud.		
Find software that can be used for sequencing.		
Make staff aware of inbuilt support in Word that can help: see TechDis Staff Pack *Benevolent Bill* for a wide range of examples; and check out **http://www.techdis.ac.uk/resources/sites/ staffpacks/index.xml**		
Provide training opportunities for staff.		
Provide touch typing support for learners such as typing programs.		
Ensure that where possible staff have access to and know how to use a digital projector and interactive whiteboards.		
Make staff and learners aware of free sources of software for text to speech such as NaturalReaders, UltraHal, Adobe Reader; see Ellen Lessner's article on TechDis at **http://www.techdis.ac.uk/?p=3_7_20050 311041158**		

Assessment

Staff should try at enrolment to identify whether candidates are likely to require support in gaining qualifications and being assessed. Such individuals can then be guided towards qualifications for which they will be able to meet the assessment requirements, either with or without support.

There is now a new chapter 2A in Part 4 of the (2002) Disability Discrimination Act (DDA) covering 'General Qualifications Bodies'. This states that examinations are covered by the DDA and therefore people cannot be treated 'less favourably on the grounds of their disability'. Examinations do need to be academically rigorous; but although standards cannot be lowered for disabled individuals, there may be different ways of assessing their competencies.

Access arrangements

Access arrangements are granted by the examining/awarding body if a candidate is likely to experience difficulty in at least one of the following areas:

> Reading
> Accuracy
> Reading speed
> Reading comprehension
> Spelling
> Handwriting speed
> Handwriting legibility
> Other difficulties associated with neurological dysfunction

Access arrangements won't automatically be granted by the awarding body if a candidate has dyslexia or learning difficulties: it will depend on:

> the effects of the difficulties during the exam and whether access arrangements will minimise these

> whether the difficulty is 'substantial'
> whether the access arrangements that the candidate needs can be allowed, given the assessment requirements of the qualification

The centre will need to decide on an appropriate arrangements, based on what will create a 'level playing field' for the candidate. If the difficulties are minor, the centre could assist by offering help with study and assessment skills.

It does not matter whether the learner has come from a school setting with a statement from an educational psychologist. A statement will not necessarily entitle the candidate to access arrangements; in fact, a diagnostic assessment that concentrates on areas of difficulty for the candidate will be more helpful.

Supporting evidence is required for learning difficulties and other disabilities where the effects of the impairment are difficult to quantify. Such evidence will usually take the form of diagnostic assessment reports, which will give the outcome of tests for reading, writing and spelling as standardised scores. These reports can be completed either by educational psychologists or by specialist teachers holding a range of approved qualifications, not only the RSA/OCR SpLD diploma.

Once the outcomes of the tests are available, the centre will need to decide – on the basis of the assessment report, its knowledge of the effects of the difficulty on the candidate and the candidate's normal way of working – what kind of support would best assist the learner.

Some special arrangements can be made at the centre's discretion. Staff can often allow extra time (usually 25% or more), rest breaks or a separate room if needed, but do check with the individual examination board. Bear in mind that if you have candidates using a laptop this may distract others, so you will need to be sensitive to everyone's needs. It is good practice to accommodate candidates using technology in a separate room.

Candidates with dyslexia may well be eligible for an amanuensis if the exam requires handwritten responses and the learner's handwriting is difficult to decipher; but generally candidates are better off using the technology they are familiar with rather than dictating responses to an unfamiliar person. Also, dictation is a difficult skill and one that need some practice. If arrangements such as an amanuensis or a reader are made, the centre is obliged to provide opportunities for the learner to practise using these arrangements.

Plan early for any examinations by sending for the booklet *Candidates with Special Assessment Needs- Special Arrangements, Regulations and Guidance*, downloadable from the Joint Council for General Qualifications website: **http://www.jcgq.org.uk/** . It contains all the necessary information.

Key points

> Practitioners have responsibilities under the DDA to make provision for all learners with disabilities.
> Look, listen and learn.
> You are not the expert on this person's dyslexia: everyone is different.
> Remember that dyslexia may run in families.
> Collect a variety of resources.
> Decide on what the tutor will do and what the organiser will do.
> Plan ahead for exams.
> Access arrangements can also cover coursework tasks, timed class activities, etc., as well as formal exams.
> Specialist assessment of some kind will be needed for access arrangements in most cases.
> It is not the class teacher or manager's role to make a decision about access arrangements: they should refer the learner to a specialist for this service, and the arrangements will be confirmed only when the awarding body has agreed them.

5

Making reading easier

Reading is essential, especially in these days of global knowledge. Where people used to be able to get most of the information they needed by asking someone, now they are likely to be using the internet or message boards to connect with a global community.

For many learners who find reading from paper hard going, the computer may be an easier medium. For a start, the text is lit from behind and many readers say they find it easier to read from the screen because it is brighter and clearer. The contrast can be adjusted more easily than on paper, and some people find that their reading and proofreading skills are more accurate when they are editing online rather than from a printout. With many packages, including standard Microsoft Office software, learners can experiment with background and foreground colours and try out all sorts of colour combinations.

Whether you are designing handouts, onscreen resources or web pages, there are many things you can do to improve the readability of your resources. It is also important to think about how the quality of the image may decrease on monitors and screens in a room with poor lighting or where reflections are apparent.

10 top tips

1 Keep electronic files of all your handouts.

2 Do not use justified text.

3 Give a choice of colours where possible.

4 Make web pages more accessible.

5 Use sans serif fonts.

6 Don't print text across images, and avoid wrap-around text.

7 Develop style sheets.

8 Do not pack in too much information.

9 Use pop-ups.

10 Provide text-to-speech facility.

1. Keep all your handouts on electronic files

In this way you will be able to change fonts and spacing easily. You can also e-mail handouts to learners which they can access on their home PCs, look at on the computer in the library, print out in a style that suits them or edit and insert their own notes – the possibilities are endless.

Have a look at the TechDis Pack *Benevolent Bill: What Microsoft Does for Accessibility* (**http://www.techdis.ac.uk/**) This pack (one of the TechDis Staff Packs) looks at the range of built-in features in Microsoft Windows and Word that either are designed to enhance accessibility or can be used creatively to make learning more accessible to certain groups.

2. Do not use justified text

With justified text (straight margins at both left and right, like newspaper columns) the spacing between the words alters from line to line to get the neat right-hand margin. Justified text is therefore harder to read than text that is aligned to the left, because it is more difficult to track text from word to word and line to line.

Tip

For some people, double spacing can also help a lot (highlight text, press Ctrl + 2). Remember, you can always put the whole document back to single spacing before you print it out (highlight text, press Ctrl + 1).

Facts about fats
About two-thirds of your brain consists of fats - specifically fatty acids. Our brain gets most of the essential fatty acids - Omega 3 and 6- from what we eat. Omega 3 fatty acids are often found in oily fish such as trout, salmon, sardine and mackerel. They can also be found in walnuts and spinach. Omega 6 fatty acids are found mainly in vegetable/nut oils, nuts, coconuts and seeds. It is worth noting that a diet should balance both Omega 6 and 3 foods. Too much Omega 6 fats can increase the risk of blood clots, heart disease and stroke.

Facts about fats
About two-thirds of your brain consists of fats - specifically fatty acids. Our brain gets most of the essential fatty acids - Omega 3 and 6- from what we eat. Omega 3 fatty acids are often found in oily fish such as trout, salmon, sardine and mackerel. They can also be found in walnuts and spinach. Omega 6 fatty acids are found mainly in vegetable/nut oils, nuts, coconuts and seeds. It is worth noting that a diet should balance both Omega 6 and 3 foods. Too much Omega 6 fats can increase the risk of blood clots, heart disease and stroke.

---

3. Give a choice of colours where possible

There is no such thing as 'one correct colour', but some dyslexic learners prefer backgrounds of pale grey, cream or pale turquoise, and some find that dark blue or dark green text is easier on the eye than black. The important thing is to give a choice where possible.

It is possible for learners with dyslexia to get specialist support to determine what their optimum colour combination may be. Dyslexia organisations can inform you of services available in the local area. The Framework for Understanding Dyslexia website (**www.dfes.gov.uk/readwriteplus/understandingdyslexia**) has a range of colour combinations based on project research.

> ## Tip
>
> Don't forget to get some coloured paper for printing out, and you could try different-coloured OHP laminate sheets to overlay pages of text in magazines or books.

4. Make web pages easier to read

The new TechDis user preferences toolbar is an excellent free resource for learners to use for reading text on web pages. It can be found at **www.techdis.ac.uk/gettoolbar** (use their search facility to find the exact page). It downloads in less than a minute and provides an extra toolbar to help learners change the font style, size and colour scheme of a website.

Valerie Schicker at Oaklands College has been assessing the TechDis toolbar with some of her learners:

'Jon prefers a blue background and finds it difficult to track print when it is too small. He found that by using the toolbar to access business sites he could read long paragraphs more easily, and he gave the colour scheme and zoom-in features 8 out of 10. He said that the toolbar is something that he would pass on to his friends as they might find it useful too; he has also downloaded it for use on his home PC.'

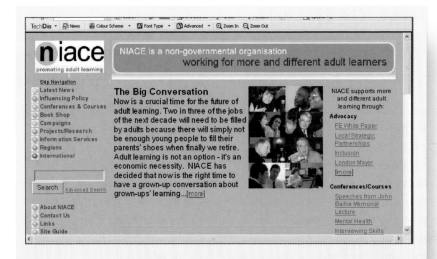

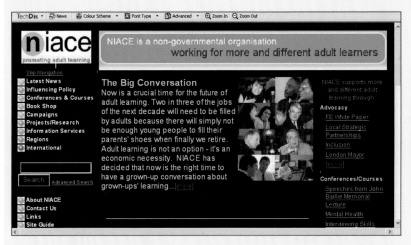

TechDis toolbar examples

5. Use sans serif fonts

Sans serif fonts such as

Comic Sans   Arial   Verdana   Tahoma

are generally recognised as being easier to read than Times Roman. Among the serif fonts, Footlight is one of the most popular as it has a distinctive upward lift on the letters, which seems to help.

Some readers have expressed a preference for fonts that have a slight slant. On the other hand, it is advisable to avoid italics, because readers with dyslexia can find these very hard to decipher and it slows down their decoding.

6. Don't print text over images

There is a fashion for watermarks and for text to be printed over images, especially in web pages. It is better to keep text and images separate. A new toolbar from Widgit called *Communicate WebWide* changes the layout of web pages to suit the needs of different learners. It separates text from images, changes the colour and style of text and puts in extra spacing. If you click on another icon it will read text aloud. **http://www.widgit.com/products/webwide/**

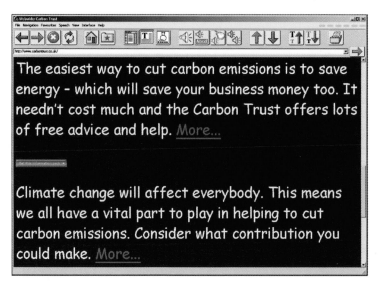

WebWide

7. Use styles and headings as signposts

With longer documents it is sometimes hard to find your way round. Tutors often insert headings and other signposts, but these can cause additional problems if not carefully thought out.

Make sure you have lots of subheadings which give the document some structure. Format these on the style box using 'Normal', 'Heading 1', 'Heading 2', etc. (see TechDis, *Benevolent Bill: What Microsoft Does for Accessibility* at **http://www.techdis.ac.uk/**)

Learners can click on View\Document Map\Outline (depending on their version of Word) and see the overall structure of the document. This way they do not have to tax their skimming and scanning skills but can get down to working on what interests them

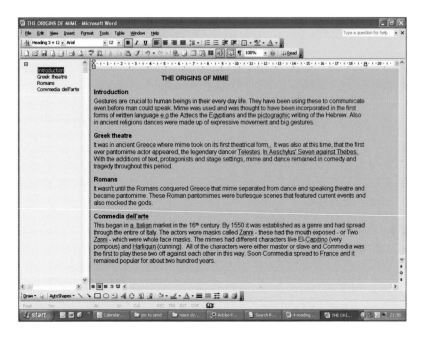

8. Do not pack in too much information

Break up your text, instead of having a long block with questions at the end. This will help those who find it hard to follow text or who lose their place easily when reading. It will also help to focus the minds of learners who find concentration a problem.

9. Use screen tips

Often screens become too busy and crowded, so a reader may not know where to start. Pop-ups let you hide the text so that learners can focus on the images or diagrams and then call up additional information when they want and need it.

Detailed instructions about screen tips can be found at:
http://www.techdis.ac.uk/resources/sites/staffpacks/index.xml
(then click on the link to 'Open Benevolent Bill - What Microsoft® does for Accessibility', and scroll down to 'Information Sheets: Screen Tips', or use the menu on the left-hand side of the screen).

Name these kitchen utensils. What is each one used for?

10. Provide a text-to-speech facility

There are many different ways of getting the computer to read text aloud. Some are free (*ReadPlease* – **http://www.readplease.com**), some use human speech with inflexions (*WordRead* – **http://www.clarosoftware.com/index.php**), and some come as part of a bigger package such as *TextHelp Read and Write Gold* (**http://www.texthelp.com**).

See the TechDis article on Free text-to-speech software: **http://www.techdis.ac.uk/?p=3_7_20050311041158**.

Tip: Headphones are a great way of ensuring privacy and avoiding distractions.

A word of warning: headphones with foam earpieces are also a good way of transmitting headlice, so encourage learners to bring their own! (You can kill lice by putting the headphones in a plastic bag in a freezer overnight.)

Useful sources of support

TechDis	See **http://www.techdis.ac.uk** – in particular the Benevolent Bill Accessibility pack
iansyst	**http://www.dyslexic.com/** has a great round-up of software
TechDis 'genres' guide	This is another excellent resource, offering a range of alternative routeways to support reading; could be direct hyperlink to **http://www.techdis.ac.uk/resources/files/ATGenres.ppt**

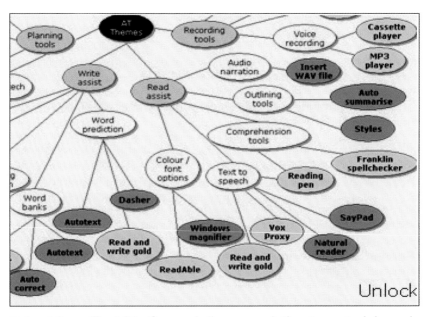

Extract from 'TechDis Genres' diagram relating to materials and methods in the TechDis Assistive Technology box training for RSCs

6

Does it have to be reading and writing?

Tutors need to think long and hard about the tasks that they set. For example, to develop or reinforce learning or aid revision or assessment, reading and writing are not necessarily essential – try to devise more creative and meaningful tasks which learners can really relate to.

Programs such as PowerPoint, Smart Notebook, Hot Potatoes and Course Genie have opened up different ways of working and have alerted managers and teaching staff to the possibility of combining text with sound, images and video to create very visual materials. Even Microsoft Word, the standard word processing package, is very versatile and can be made interactive by using tables, creating forms and working with hyperlinks.

Many relevant materials and training activities can be found in the E-Guide training packs, and materials for professional development are being developed through 2006 for use on the Staff Development e-learning Centre (SDELC). Material for review and evaluation can be accessed via **http://www.sdelc.co.uk/**

Working with the text

There are lots of things you can do with Word. You can:

> underline words
> pick out points with a highlighter
> make forms that have drop-down boxes containing the answers:

Use the highlighter to pick out 5 key facts

A Brief Description of Mumming
Mummers plays were originally part of the old fertility rites performed in mid-winter and the May Day festivals to bring back life to the world. They almost always have a cycle of death, followed by resurrection. This cycle involves a fight between the hero (usually St George) and the villain, who can vary. In the combat play we perform, the villain is Bold Slasher-The Turkish Knight.

The corpse is then brought back to life by the Doctor, after which there are appearances by other characters, most having only tenuous links with the story line, and usually used as a means of extracting money from the audience. Mummers plays are usually humorous and in rhyme, and although traditionally performed only by men. There are in the region of 1000 Mummers plays in existence in Britain.

Using the highlighter

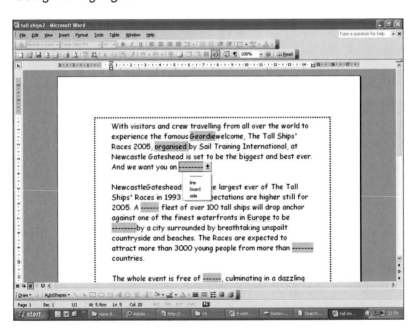

Drop-down boxes

Diagrams *v.* text

Some people do like having a block of text to work with, but we are all becoming more visually aware, largely because of the way information is presented to us these days. From websites to street signs and hoardings, the world bombards us with pictures and symbols.

All learners benefit from text being broken up into smaller chunks, and many people work better with a more pictorial approach. Compare these two examples:

How do I make up a bottle?

There are a few key rules you need to follow if you are going to make up formula milk:

Always put the water in the bottle first to make sure that you are using the right amount of water|

Follow the manufacturers' guidelines regarding how much formula to put in one bottle –

Overfill each scoop and then scrape off the excess to make sure you have the right amount of formula Always shake or stir the bottle and test the temperature before serving.

Always test the temperature of the bottle by dripping some of the milk onto the inside of your wrist.

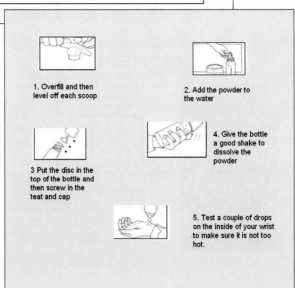

1. Overfill and then level off each scoop

2. Add the powder to the water

3 Put the disc in the top of the bottle and then screw in the teat and cap

4. Give the bottle a good shake to dissolve the powder

5. Test a couple of drops on the inside of your wrist to make sure it is not too hot.

Keep instructions simple

Think about providing instructions in written form, using bullet points so that learners can find exactly where they are and see what they should do next:

> # Your task
>
> - Open a PowerPoint presentation
> - Insert a title slide
> - Put the title: Cereal Packets
> - Save
> - Insert two blank slides
> - Insert a photograph of the front and back of a selected cereal (from your CD)
> - Fill in the worksheet (optional!)
> - Create a reporting back presentation on a blank slide or by pasting into a Text and Content Layout slide.

Combine different media

PowerPoint slides are a good way of combining pictures, text and sound. This example from materials about Martin Luther King combines sound files, key quotations, headlines and photographs:

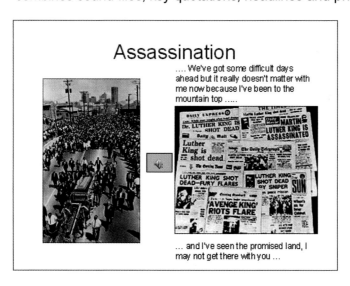

Make it easy to follow: gather together web resources together on one page to give easy access. This is particularly useful if learners are likely to mis-type web addresses and so not be able to access pages:

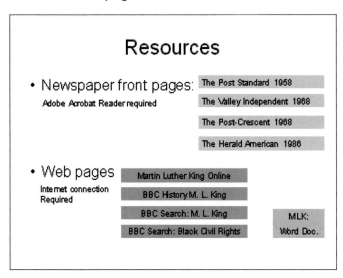

Go for short answers:

Sorting activities

Barry is in his 50s. He is a learner with dyslexia who has been attending Skills for Life sessions for two years. On some days his reading is better than on others. Spelling and punctuation are an obstacle, and he is embarrassed by his lack of progress in this area.

He is fascinated by music hall, so his tutor Rob suggested that he do a presentation on the subject. Barry liked this idea because it didn't involve too much writing. Rob suggested that Barry put together a plan before he started, but this did not work for him. Instead, he used the Internet for research and wrote all over his printouts. Then he went into PowerPoint and copied and pasted text and graphics from a range of websites. Once he had assembled a lot of pages (about 40) he used the slide sorter view to rearrange them, deleting some, combining others and expanding some of the text. This visual way of sorting suited him well.

Using PowerPoint as a visual prompt

PowerPoint can work well as a photo album and can provide key points and clues for listeners and speakers alike:

Song Karn Festival in Thailand

- Traditional Thai New Year
- April 13- April 15
- Food for the monks
- Releasing fishes and birds
- Blessings
- The importance of water

Labelling diagrams

Labelling can help learners show what they know; it can also provide useful materials they can easily revise from:

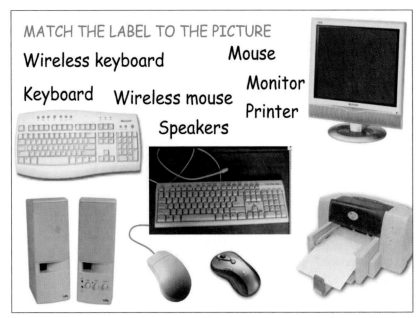

MATCH THE LABEL TO THE PICTURE

Wireless keyboard   Mouse

Keyboard   Wireless mouse   Monitor

Speakers   Printer

Labelling activity

Cloze

Activities such as cloze, where learners work through a passage from which certain words or phrases are omitted, can be a good way for them to familiarise themselves with the content and language of different curriculum areas. It is particularly good for those for whom English is their first language.

It is important that the tutor scaffolds such activities carefully, especially in the early stages. That said, cloze can be a good way of learning, revising and demonstrating knowledge, and can be as easy or challenging as the tutor wants to make it.

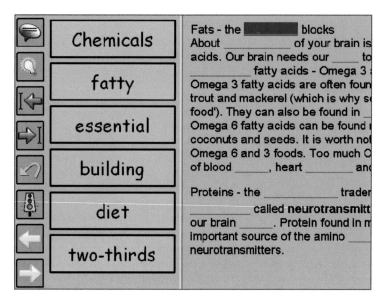

Chemicals

fatty

essential

building

diet

two-thirds

Fats - the [blocks] blocks
About _____ of your brain is
acids. Our brain needs our _____ to
_____ fatty acids - Omega 3 ;
Omega 3 fatty acids are often foun
trout and mackerel (which is why s
food'). They can also be found in _
Omega 6 fatty acids can be found i
coconuts and seeds. It is worth not
Omega 6 and 3 foods. Too much O
of blood _____, heart _____ an

Proteins - the _____ trader
_____ called **neurotransmitt**
our brain _____. Protein found in m
important source of the amino _____
neurotransmitters.

Drag and drop

Often by moving things around, a kinaesthetic learner will find
ways of learning and remembering that are much more effective
than working purely with text:

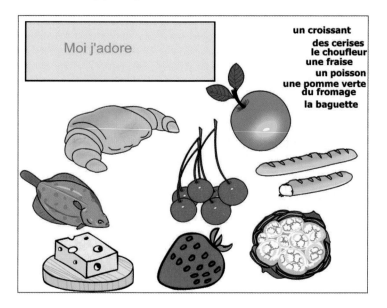

Moi j'adore

un croissant
des cerises
le choufleur
une fraise
un poisson
une pomme verte
du fromage
la baguette

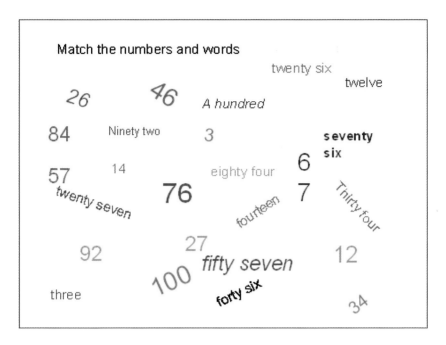

Match the numbers and words

Webquest

A webquest is a good way of moving learners on from short activities to longer projects. Webquests present a set of questions and guidance for completing the task. Often learners co-operate and work together on a webquest, using their listening and speaking skills to work with partners or present to large groups. Some people find this less threatening than individual work.

Webquests are quite taxing because they require learners to go beyond reading and remembering, encouraging them to engage in higher-order thinking, where they apply, synthesise, analyse and evaluate. This plays to the strengths shown by many people with dyslexia.

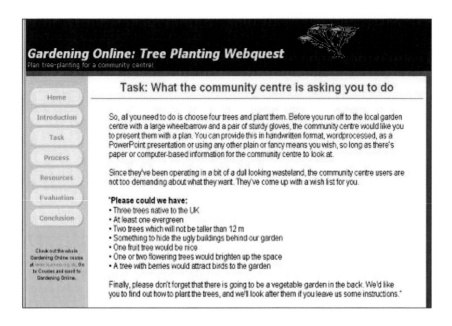

Think about how you could use some of these activities with your learners:

Ideas	Uses
Highlight/underline key points	
Copy and paste significant information	
Ask learners to present ideas as bullet points	
Drag and drop images and text	
Take photographs	
Take videos	
Make sound clips	
Give short answers	
Sort slides	
Label diagrams	
Cloze	
Webquest	
Games	

Further information

On the 'Creation of learning materials' section of the TechDis website (**http://www.techdis.ac.uk/?p=9_7**) there are lots of suggestions for using audio and video images, plus accessibility pros and cons – well worth logging on to.

7

Supporting writing

Writing takes place in four stages:

1 Gathering ideas and information
2 Deciding what to use and in which order
3 Getting the words on the paper
4 Checking it for mistakes

Nearly every piece of guidance about writing has the same advice:

> Make a plan
> Flesh it out
> Write a draft
> Revise it
> Proofread

Plan–Draft–Revise is a very traditional left-brain approach to writing. More importantly, it is based on a handwriting model. Word processing has now changed the way we write. Many people now compose directly on to a word processor and so can cut-and-paste or drag-and-drop text and images without making their work messy or hard to follow.

Planning

It is often a good idea to get learners to talk about what they want their work to be like – or, better still, to record their ideas on tape as a prompt and as evidence of the planning process. Post-its or mind maps can be used to gather, expand and develop ideas, and some tutors recommend using the Outline tool in Word so that headings and their underlying text can be easily reordered.

Writing

When using a word processor, people tend to write more because it is less of an effort. They can alter a piece of text time and again without having to rewrite or retype their work. This puts them in control. Do they want to correct spellings as they go along by right-clicking on the word, or wait till the end and do a spell check over the whole document?

Because the word processor minimises spelling and handwriting problems, students feel free to concentrate on the ideas and how they want to express them. This encourages them to be more adventurous in their use of language and syntax.

Speech facility aids

Learners who do not have the necessary visual skills to distinguish between different spellings will benefit from packages that incorporate a speech facility, enabling them to hear synonymous words before choosing the one they want. Some people like the homophone checker in TextHelp's *Read and Write Gold* (**http://www.texthelp.com**) – others find this confusing, as it alerts them to similar sounding words that have never caused them problems before!

Keyboards

Using a keyboard often makes it easier for people with motor integration problems to write things down. The text produced by a word processor is legible, and readers will not make assumptions about the writer based upon the appearance of the work.

Practitioners can help dyslexic learners by making the keyboard easier to see. A keyboard such as Big Keys (**http://www.iansyst.co.uk/**) may help them find the keys more quickly and with less effort; those with a knowledge of a keyboard might prefer a simplified keyboard, a flat keyboard (Alu-Mini) or a 'cherry keyboard' (**http://www.iansyst.co.uk/**). Centres might also consider investing in touch typing packages (**http://www.iansyst.co.uk/**).

Many people with dyslexia write so slowly that their brains race ahead while their writing lags behind. This can affect the composition process. Learning to use the correct fingers (touch-typing), some discover patterns on the keyboard – the word 'was' forms a triangle on the keypad; 'were' is three steps forward and one back. This kinaesthetic approach helps: touch is added to sight and sound.

Writing frames

Writing frames provide 'scaffolding'. The grid may contain individual words that the user finds hard to spell – e.g. *accommodation, accessible, separately* – or specialist words – *particle, soluble, photosynthesis, reactivity*. It can also provide a framework for composing sentences and developing the right tone or style. For example, persuasive writing requires a different approach from discursive or analytical writing.

> Margaret is from Jamaica. Now in her sixties, she lives in Wolverhampton and finds her dyslexia more of an obstacle than ever before. Her niece Naomi has gone back to the West Indies, and all the family over there are keen to have regular news. Margaret wants to be able to send e-mails. It's not just her spelling – she has no idea what sort of things people say in e-mails. So her tutor Keith spent time drafting her first e-mail. From this he has put together some phrases and headings to make a writing frame in WordBar (**http://www.cricksoft.com/**).

These words/phrases give Margaret a mental map of the sorts of things she should think about – what she has been doing, who she has seen, news of the family and friends at the West Indian Club. Margaret has now started to keep a diary where she jots things down so she has more news to send.

Some learners will benefit from a predictive word processor or a word list facility so that they can select words they frequently use rather than typing them out each time, thereby decreasing the chances of error.

Whereas a grid requires an input from a teacher or another good speller, predictive word processors start from an enormous bank of words which appear in a little window as the user starts typing the first letter. The most popular programs are TextHelp Read and Write Gold; Penfriend, Co:writer.

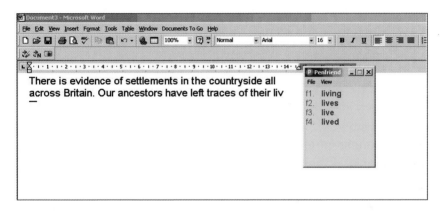

Voice recognition aids

Voice recognition programs such as Dragon Naturally Speaking are another useful tool for learners with dyslexia. The principle behind this is that you speak, and it types: spoken words are translated into text.

It requires a lot of time and training to get to a reasonable level of accuracy, but some learners believe find that even without complete accuracy it is better for them than typing.

Tip
Make sure learners realise that, even though a word may correctly spelled via a voice recognition program, it still may not be the right word.

Speech recognition needs to be used alongside a text reader. Users need to learn some dictation skills, too. They need to learn how to vocalise punctuation and speak without interruption, as all 'ums' and 'ers' will appear in the text.

Thomas uses a voice recorder to take notes, and for many years has relied on his wife to act as an amanuensis – 'I have the words, I just cannot get them written down myself.' Speech recognition software had an immediate appeal for Thomas, and he was undaunted by the training and enrolment process. His wife was even more enthusiastic.

Speech feedback for proofreading

In many cases speech feedback is even more useful than voice recognition. Users can hear what they have written, and this helps them identify any mistakes.

An awareness of errors is the first step towards improving skills. For example, if they type *'the dinning room'* they will hear immediately that they have made a mistake. They can then experiment with alternative spellings or consult a spell checker.

Sound is invaluable for students who confuse the letters *b* and *d*, since they will often hear the difference when the word is read out. Some learners find that sound can help them to improve their punctuation skills as they can hear the different emphases given to their writing by inserting or removing commas or moving punctuation around in a text.

Speech can also help in those cases where the learner has typed in the wrong word:

Humphrey Bogart stared in Casablanca

Since *'stared'* is correctly spelled it would not be picked up by a spell checker, but the writer can hear that it is wrong.

Some learners find that speech feedback helps them become aware of repetitious phrasing in their work:

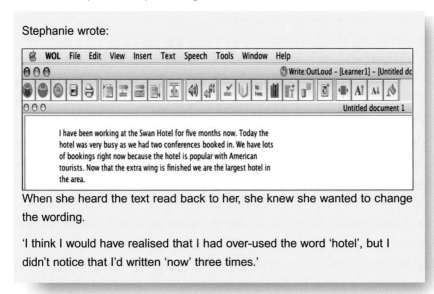

Stephanie wrote:

I have been working at the Swan Hotel for five months now. Today the hotel was very busy as we had two conferences booked in. We have lots of bookings right now because the hotel is popular with American tourists. Now that the extra wing is finished we are the largest hotel in the area.

When she heard the text read back to her, she knew she wanted to change the wording.

'I think I would have realised that I had over-used the word 'hotel', but I didn't notice that I'd written 'now' three times.'

Points to consider

> Encourage learners to move beyond the traditional Plan–Draft–Revise model.

> Use spell checkers, especially those with additional speech facilities.

> Keyboarding can make a difference to speed and confidence.

> Touch typing brings in a kinaesthetic element.

> Writing frames can help with composition and difficult spellings.

> Predictive word processing and voice recognition can speed up composition for some learners, but require a considerable investment of time and training.

> Speech feedback provides auditory support for proofreading.

> Technology helps because it gives users different tools to try out.

> There is no magic solution – some facilities will work well for one individual but not for another.

Other aids to consider

Also see the TechDis 'genres' guide, which offers a range of alternative routeways to support writing:
http://www.techdis.ac.uk/resources/files/ATGenres.ppt

8

Good skills for learners

Of course, the same learners will not continue to come to your classes – or at least, we hope not! They need to be learning skills and then progressing to *new* courses and developing *new* interests. Part of your role as a tutor should be to give them the confidence to become more independent learners.

Here are some useful skills. Try these yourself so you are confident before you pass them on to learners:

> Changing colours and fonts
> Paste special
> AutoSummarise
> Highlight
> Spike
> Turn into bullet points
> Spelling
> Thesaurus
> Make autocorrect entry
> Google toolbar

Sam has found that using technology has helped his confidence and his literacy skills. He makes good use of a spell checker, has developed autocorrect entries for words he has real problems with. He can change the appearance of the Window – background colour and font colour (white on red) – and return it to standard settings when he has finished.
Tutor, Staffordshire

How to change colours and fonts

The easiest way to do this in Word, or in an e-mail using Word as its editor, is to click on 'Format\Background' and pick a colour. This may not *print out* in colour, but is an aid to reading messages on-screen.

Change the style and colour of the font by clicking on 'Format\Font', then on the arrow under 'Font colour' to open up the palette of text colours.

Tip

To make a more permanent change, select 'Start\Control panel\Display – Appearance'. Under 'Windows and buttons', choose 'Windows Classic Style' and play with the colour schemes. If you are on a network, see if you can link preferences to a user name.

Paste special

Sometimes learners want to download information from the web but just want the words so they can pick out the main points. Here's how to do it:

Highlight text in the web page, then Copy\Open Word\Edit\Paste special\Unformatted text; paste on to the new page, and you have all the text on one page to work with, without any extraneous material (graphics, etc.).

AutoSummarise

Get a quick summary of any document in Word. Open a Word document. Select Tools\ AutoSummarise; choose '25%', '50%' or 'Pick out key points'. AutoSummarise scans the document and finds the words that are used most frequently. It then gives a score to each sentence.

This is very effective on well structured documents such as reports, but is pretty hopeless on more creative stuff.

Highlighter

This is on the formatting toolbar and looks quite like a highlighter. Click on the icon, or on the arrow next to it to select a different colour. Then as you run the tool over the words, they get a highlighted background. If you change your mind, run the highlighter over the words again and the colour disappears.

This is good for picking out the main points of a text.

THE ORIGINS OF MIME

Gestures are crucial to human beings in their every day life. They have been using these to communicate even before man could speak. Mime was used and was thought to have been incorporated in the first forms of written language e.g the Aztecs the Egyptians and the pictograghic writing of the Hebrew. **Also in ancient religions dances were made up of expressive movement and big gestures.**

It was in ancient Greece where mime took on its first theatrical form. It was also at this time, that the first ever pantomime actor appeared, the legendary dancer Telestes. In Aeschylus' Seven against Thebes he acted out every word the chorus spoke and danced through every song that they sang without the use of a single word. **With the additions of text, protagonists and stage settings, mime and dance remained in comedy and tragedy throughout this period. It wasn't until the Romans conquered Greece that mime separated from dance and speaking theatre and became pantomime.** These Roman pantomimes were burlesque scenes that featured current events and also mocked the gods.

Spike

This is a really useful but little known tool. Highlight the relevant point in a document. Press 'Control' + F3 and the text will disappear. **Do not panic!** Continue to do this until you have selected and cut out all the relevant details. Open a new document and press 'Shift' and 'Control + F3' and all the text reappears on your new page. This is a great way to collect together lots of points from different documents while the ideas are fresh in your mind.

> ### A word of warning!
> Once you have cut all the good bits out of a document, the program will ask if you want to save changes. **Say no** to keep the original document unchanged – otherwise you will lose everything that you have just cut out of it.

Using bullet points or numbering

This is a good thinking tool. Somehow it is easier to re-order and expand points than fragments of text.

Drag and drop the main points, or position the cursor before each 'point' and press 'Enter' to move it to a fresh line. Then highlight the text to be bulleted and click on the bullet point icon (or the numbering icon next to it) and the software puts in the bullets or numbers to give them emphasis.

Spell checker

Everyone needs this! In many word processing packages, when the computer does not recognise a word it will put a red line underneath it. If you click the right-hand button on your mouse, a list of suggestions pops up.

You can also choose to check the spellings in the whole document. Click on 'Tools' on the Menu bar, then choose 'Spelling'. Some computers also bring up the spell checker when you press the F7 key, or click on the 'Spelling & Grammar' (ABC) icon on the toolbar.

When the computer finds a word that it thinks is spelled wrong it will stop, show you that word and display a list of suggestions. If the word you want is in the list, select it with the mouse and click 'Change'. Learners can go back and spell-check the whole paper when they get to the end of it, or, by right-clicking any word underlined in red, they can check their spelling as they go along.

One of the good things about spell checkers is that they stop people dithering over spellings and prevent them from changing correctly spelled words. Many learners report that their spelling has improved as a result of spell checkers, as the same mistakes are highlighted again and again.

Remember that some learners will need a spell checker that reads the words out.

Thesaurus

The thesaurus is a great tool for finding the meanings of words and extending vocabulary.

Try this activity:

Type the following words: *narrative*; *overwhelmed*; *instigate*. Highlight each in turn and press Shift + F7. Synonyms (and in some cases antonyms) will appear in a new window

'If you don't know how to spell *obtain*, type *get* and use the Thesaurus.'
Learner in Leicester

From the very beginnings of human occupation of sites right through diverse time periods, we will investigate and examine our ancestors' way of living through material remains. It is by analysing these sites of past habitation that we may learn and understand our own cultural past and what it means to us today.

From traditional methods, such as field walking and artefact recognition, right through the spectrum to aerial photography, satellite remote sensing and virtual computer reconstruction, you will discover and unravel the exciting mysteries of the past.

Search for:
spectrum
Thesaurus: English (U.K.)
Back
Thesaurus: English (U.K.)
range (n.)
range
band
field
gamut
variety
scale
continuum
Can't find it?
Try one of these alternatives or see Help for hints on refining your search

AutoCorrect

AutoCorrect on the tools menu in Word is a great way of writing longer words – 'accom' expands to 'accommodation', 'govt' to 'government'. Learners can get on with what they are saying instead of always thinking at word level.

Click on the 'Tools' menu and choose 'AutoCorrect'. Type the abbreviation in the left-hand column and the full word in the right.

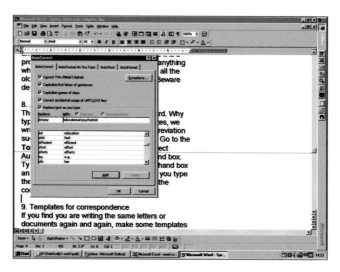

Choose 'Add' and 'OK'; then, forever after, each time you type the abbreviation and press the space bar, it will write out the word in full.

Google toolbar

Your learners are going to want to access a lot of information from the web. Those with dyslexia may find it problematic to type in their phone numbers and e-mail addresses accurately – and these are essentials for e-bay, Amazon and other online commerce.

The Google toolbar (**http://toolbar.google.com**) has several useful functions. Sometimes learners type in a search term and then when the page opens they can't find what they are looking for. If they click on the highlighter tool, every instance of the search term will be picked out in a bright colour. It also has a spell checker which works with web-based mail.

The final benefit is the Autofill facility. You fill in your details just once. Then when a form comes up on screen, any fields that turn yellow can be filled in automatically by clicking on the Autofill tool. It will then fill in your name, address, email and phone number. It could even fill in your credit card details for you.

N.B.: It is always wise to consider the security issues of giving out credit card details, especially in centres where there may be little privacy.

9

Conclusion

You have worked with your learner for a number of months. You have discussed issues, options and ways of working at an initial interview. You have identified strengths and created a range of materials that will work well for this individual, and possibly for other learners too. You have moved away from a text-based delivery and looked at visual, auditory and kinaesthetic approaches that have more to offer to learners with dyslexia, and you have considered the value of adopting strategies that work for right-brain individuals. You have identified potential obstacles to delivery and assessment and found ways of maximising achievement. What next?

The important thing is to move the learner on. People with dyslexia may lack confidence in their abilities. The challenge for the tutor is to promote a learning environment where learners can become confident that they can use the approaches they have been taught, to move on – into further learning or employment, or simply to make their leisure activities more fun.

'I'd never really used a computer before. We've got a computer at home and my husband's always used it. I was a bit afraid of it, to be honest. Then I started coming down here. Because it was a drop-in centre and there's no specific time to come and you don't have to stay the whole time, gradually it built my confidence up.

I'm now doing exams in computers, and each time I go to do the exam or part of the course, I'm astonished at how well I'm doing. I didn't realise I could do it and or that I would remember. Each time I go away, I come back and think, 'Gosh I can remember it!'

I'm really surprised at my own ability to use the computer and at my confidence. I want to move on now to a more advanced class and get more qualifications. There's nothing to stop me now.' *Carolyn, Warwickshire*

10

References

Organisations

AbilityNet
http://www.abilitynet.co.uk/

Adult Dyslexia Organisation
http://www.futurenet.co.uk/charity/ado/adomenu/adomenu.htm

Becta
http://www.becta.org.uk/

British Dyslexia Association
http://www.bdadyslexia.org.uk/

Dyslexia Institute
http://www.dyslexia-inst.org.uk/

National Literacy Trust
http://www.literacytrust.org.uk/

NIACE
http://www.niace.org.uk/

Patoss
http://www.patoss-dyslexia.org/

TechDis
http://www.techdis.ac.uk/

Sites

aclearn Technology and Dyslexia
http://www.aclearn.net/display.cfm?page=1061

A Framework for Understanding Dyslexia
http://www.dfes.gov.uk/readwriteplus/understandingdyslexia

Disability Rights Commission
http://www.drc-gb.org/

Disability Discrimination Act
http://www.opsi.gov.uk/acts/acts1995/1995050.htm

OCR
http://www.ocr.org.uk OCR's access assessment regulations, for both vocational and general qualifications can be found on OCR's website in the section devoted to Exams Officers.

Staff Development e-learning Centre (SDELC)
As of June 2006, this site is under development. Well worth a visit to get an idea of how materials are developing:
http://www.sdelc.co.uk/

TechDis   TechDis aims to be the leading educational advisory service, working across the UK, in the fields of accessibility and inclusion:
http://www.techdis.ac.uk

Staff packs are particularly useful:
http://www.techdis.ac.uk/resources/sites/staffpacks/index.x ml

Books and articles

Backhouse, Gill, Dolman, Elizabeth and Read, Caroline (2005). *Dyslexia: Assessing the Need for Access Arrangements during Examinations: A Practical Guide*, 2nd edition Evesham: PATOSS, in conjunction with JCQ.

Davis, Ronald D. and Braun, Eldon M. (1997). *The Gift of Dyslexia: Why Some of the Brightest People Can't Read and How They Can Learn*. London: Souvenir Press.

DfES (2004). A *Framework for Understanding Dyslexia*. London: DfES.

Kirk, J. and Reid, G. (2001). An examination of the relationship between dyslexia and offending in young people and the implications for the training system. *Dyslexia*, vol. 7, no. 2.

Krupska, M. and Klein, C. (1995) *Demystifying Dyslexia*. London: Hodder & Stoughton for London Language and Literacy Unit.

Squires, Garry and McKeown, Sally (2006). *Supporting Children with Dyslexia*. London: Continuum International.

Sunderland, Helen, Klein, Cynthia, Savinson, Rosemary and Partridge, Tracy (1997). *Dyslexia and the Bilingual Learner.* London: London Language and Literacy Unit, South Bank University.

Contacts for software mentioned in the text

Company	Address	Type of software
ClaroView http://www.clarosoftware.com	Claro Software Ltd Premier House Office 27, Church Street Preston, Lancashire PR1 3BQ 01870 760 5877	Software to magnify, change settings or alter the appearance of text to make it easier to read
Course Genie www.horizonwimba.com	Sentry House 110b Northgate Street Bury St Edmunds Suffolk IP33 1HP 01284 747780	Open-ended software to create learning activities
Crick http://www.cricksoft.com	Crick Software Ltd Crick House Boarden Close Moulton Park Northampton NN3 6LF 01604 671691	Writing support and multimedia tools Clicker/ ClozePro; WordBar
don Johnston http://www.donjohnston.co.uk	Don Johnston Special Needs Ltd 18/19 Clarendon Court Calver Road Winwick Quay Warrington, WA2 8QP 01925 256500	Talking word processors, predictive word processors, planning tools: Co:Writer/ Draft:Builder/ Write:Outloud/ Start to Finish
Hot Potatoes http://hotpot.uvic.ca/	A free download which can be used to create non-profit activities for any organisation	Makes interactive quizzes, multiple-choice, crosswords matching/ordering and gap-fill exercises

Software	Contact	Description
iansyst http://www.dyslexic.com	iansyst Ltd Fen House Fen Road, Cambridge CB4 1UN 01223 426644	Dyslexia specialists supplying hardware and software
inclusive technology http://www.inclusive.co.uk/	Inclusive Technology Ltd Gatehead Business Park Delph New Road Delph, Oldham OL3 5BX 01457 819790	Note takers and software to support reading and writing
PenFriend http://www.penfriend.ltd.uk	PenFriend Ltd 30 South Oswald Road Edinburgh EH9 2HG 0131 668 2000	A predictive package that works well with Microsoft Word
Smart Notebook http://www.smart-education.org/uk	Christ Church University Canterbury, Kent CT1 1QU 01227 782802	Software for interactive whiteboards; can be downloaded free of charge
TextHelp http://www.texthelp.com	TextHelp Systems Ltd Enkalon Business Centre 25 Randalstown Road Antrim, Northern Ireland BT41 4LJ 0800 328 7910	Dyslexia software for text-to-speech, homophone checkers, prediction, speaking calculator, speaking phonetic spell checker, etc.
Widgit http://www.widgit.com	Widgit Software Ltd 124 Cambridge Science Park, Milton Rd, Cambridge CB4 0ZS 01223 425 558	A company that specialises in symbol software, Widgit also has Communicate: Webwide, which will change the layout and appearance of web pages
Words Worldwide http://www.keyspell.net	Words Worldwide Ltd Ash House Bell Villas Ponteland Newcastle Upon Tyne NE20 9BE 01661 860999	Distributes software for dyslexia support including screen readers, voice recognition software, typing tutors

>> More e-guidelines

Guidance and support, accessible advice and useful examples of good practice for adult learning practitioners who want to use digital technology in all its forms to attract and support adult learners.

All e-guidelines are £9.95, US$20.00, €17.00, but there is a special offer:

NEW for 2006

e-guidelines 1
Online resources in the classroom
Using the World Wide Web to deliver and support adult learning
Alan Clarke and Claudia Hesse
ISBN 1 86201 224 5, 2005, 60pp,

e-guidelines 2
Digital cameras in teaching and learning
Phil Hardcastle
ISBN 1 86201 225 3, 2005, 36pp,

e-guidelines 3
Developing e-learning materials
Applying user-centred design
Shubhanna Hussain
ISBN 1 86201 226 1, 2005, 48pp,

e-guidelines 4
e-learning in outreach
Glyn Owen and Khawar Iqbal
ISBN 1 86201 227 X, 2005, 56pp,

e-guidelines 5
e-learning and modern foreign language teaching
Jacky Elliott
ISBN 1 86201 229 6, January 2006, 56pp,

e-guidelines 6
Integrating ICT Skill for Life with financial education
Alan Clarke
ISBN 1 86201 275 X, March 2006, 64pp,

e-guidelines 7
Attracting and motivating new learners with ICT
Jackie Essom
ISBN 1 86201 276 8, May 2006, 64pp,

e-guidelines 8
e-learning for teaching English for Speakers of Other Languages
Mary Moss and Sue Southwood
ISBN 1 86201 228 8, March 2006, 64pp

To order, contact NIACE, Publications Sales, Renaissance House, 20 Princess Road West, Leicester LE1 6TP.

Tel. 0116 204 4215, Email: orders@niace.org.uk
Or visit our website at www.niace.org/publications